On Your Way...

Words of wisdom and encouragement for those about to embark on a new journey in life.

Stephanie Edwards

ISBN: Softcover   978-1-7960-3126-3
         Hardcover   978-1-7960-3127-0
         EBook   978-1-7960-3125-6

To order additional copies of this book, contact:
Xlibris
1-888-795-4274
www.Xlibris.com
Orders@Xlibris.com

Print information available on the last page

Rev. date: 04/30/2019

This book is dedicated to my son, Dylan, the boy who gave me the title of Mom. May you always be true to yourself and realize that the world is a much brighter place because you are in it. May you feel confident in the continued evolution of you in this world and always know how much you are loved.

Your big day is here
you've paid all your dues,
the world is your oyster
just waiting for you.

You're just starting out
on the road that you choose,
the sky is the limit
no time for the blues.

As you head out
on the path of your choice
let the world feel your presence
and the sound of your voice.

Let your hard work ethic
and knowledge combine.
Show the world what you're made of
and you'll get along fine.

Whether you're in the city
or on the country farm,
make the world take notice
with your wit and your charm.

Always remember to help others
and try to do no harm.
Make impacts both big and small
and don't sleep past your alarm.

Don't spread yourself too thin,
you won't be at your best.
Choose your efforts wisely
and take notice of the rest.

Give back to your community
and help it to be strong.
Encourage help from others
to see the projects along.

Take time for the beauty
of the world so bright and sunny
and when it comes to work
chase the dream, not the money.

Learn to save your money,
your time and preserve
for you never know when
you need to pull from reserves.

Remember to call home
and let them know you care,
tell them of your journeys
and take the time to share.

Get back to your roots
every now and then,
as life can take you off track
and family can get you back in.

Take pictures of your life
as you will forget along the way.
Take time to reminisce
all the glory of each day.

Thank God for your blessings
and your parents for their heart,
for you are all grown up now
but they gave you your start.

Give credit where it is due
and praise when it is needed.
Be strong in your conviction
but do not be conceited.

Be truthful, be kind,
be humble, be bold, be brave
and when in the presence of others
always remember behave.

Lead by example
and not just in words you say.
Be a leader for others
who need help to find their way.

And when you put your head down
on your pillow to rest
remember life's a journey
and always do your best.

Printed in the United States
By Bookmasters